Ulises Wensell
Josep Mª Parramón

autumn

Parramón

The green leaves of summer

change to the golden colours of autumn

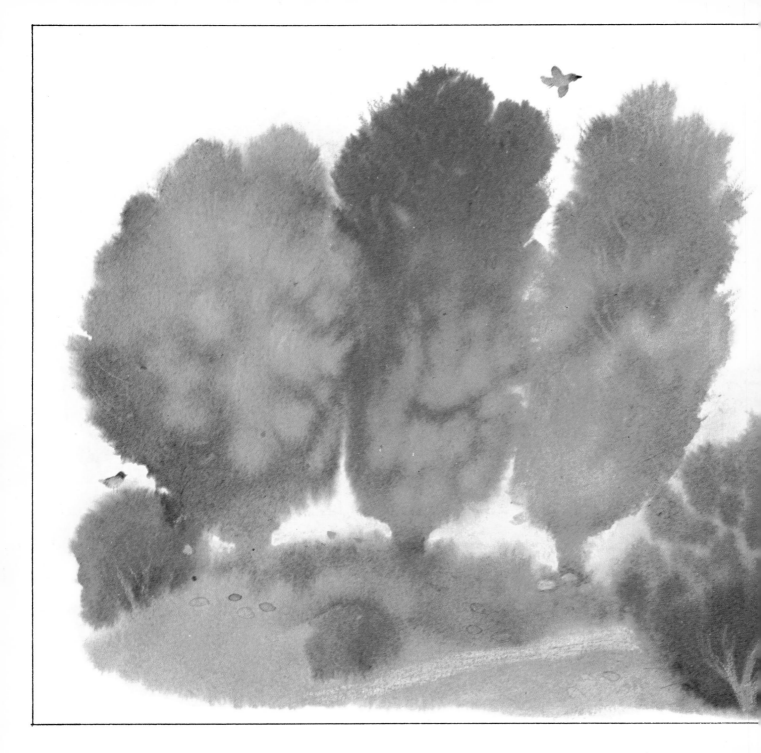

The leaves turn red, yellow, brown, orange and scarlet before they fall

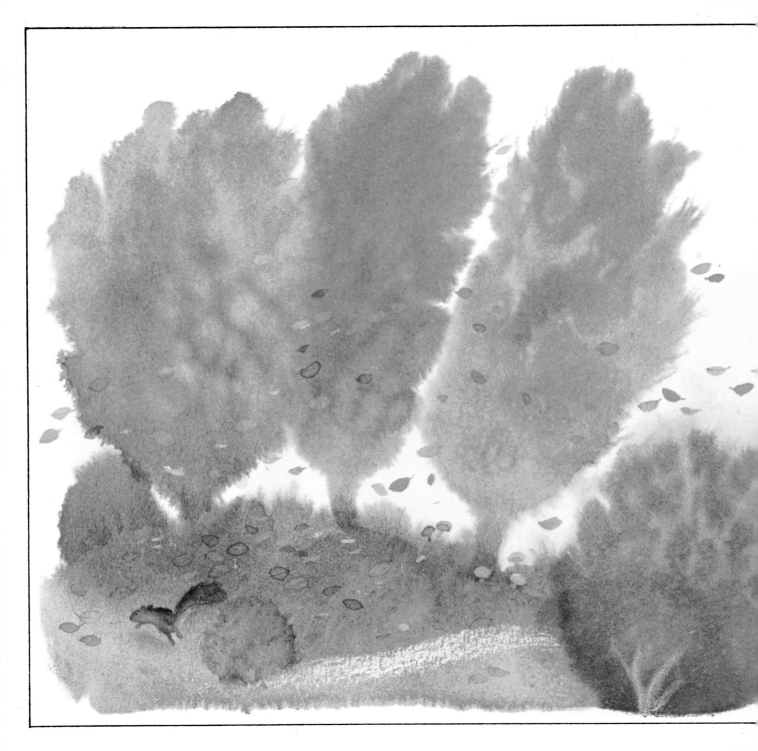

Slowly the trees lose their leaves

The weather is very changeable

...the rain comes suddenly

The holidays are over

It's time to go back to school

Back to homework in the long evenings

It gets dark earlier

It's fun to splash in the puddles

Autumn is the season for making wine

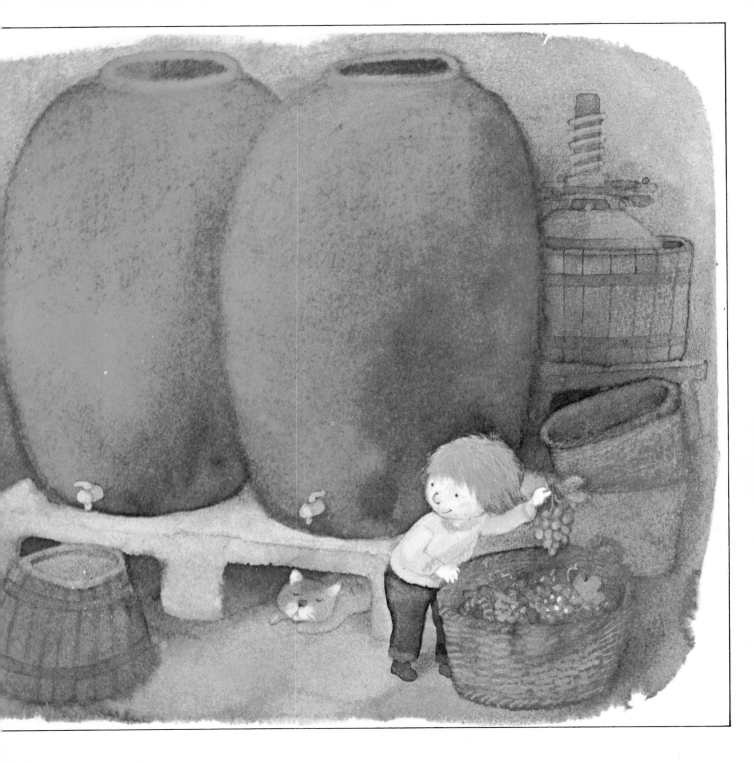

...and Granny makes lots of lovely jams

It's autumn!

AUTUMN

The change of season means a change of colours
Autumn is a wonderful time — in no other season is there such a dramatic change in the colours of nature. The green tones of summertime turn to russet, red, orange, gold and brown in October and November until the leaves fall.

The weather gets colder and birds fly south
After the blue skies of summer there is more rain and the temperature drops. The swallows who arrived in the late spring now fly home to the warm south.

Autumn is the season for hunting
In the countryside the hunting season begins. The hounds chase the fox and the rabbit. Huntsmen take their rifles to shoot game — partridge, pheasant and deer.

The farmers start again
The crops are harvested and the fields cleared ready for ploughing. The soil is fertilised and prepared for new seed to be sown.